Exploring Physical Science

Exploring

SOUND, LIGHT, AND RADIATION

Andrew Solway

rosen publishing's
rosen central

New York

Published in 2008 by The Rosen Publishing Group, Inc.
29 East 21st Street, New York, NY 10010

First Edition

Cover photograph: Dane Wirtzfeld/istockphoto.com

Photo credits: p. 4: Clive Rose/Getty Images; p. 6: Thomas Mounsey/istockphoto.com;
p. 9: Ed Parker/EASI-Images/cfwimages.com; p. 11: Michael Langhals/istockphoto.com;
p. 12: Photographer's Mate 3rd Class Chris Thamaan/U.S. Navy; p. 14: Bo Veisland,
MI&I/Science Photo Library; p. 16: Photographer's Mate Airman Chris Valdez/U.S. Navy;
p. 19: Laura Frenkel/istockphoto.com; p. 20: Andrea Gingerich/istockphoto.com; p. 21: Peter
Llewellyn/istockphoto.com; p. 22: Library of Congress; p. 23: Hsianyu Kuo/istockphoto.com;
p. 24: Matteo Natale/istockphoto.com; p. 25: Professor Dan Z. Reinstein/London Vision Clinic;
p. 28: NOAA Photo Library/ NOAA Central Library, (OAR/ERL/National Severe Storms
Laboratory); p. 29: Doris Ulmann/Library of Congress; p. 30: Brian Stanback/istockphoto.com;
p. 31: Nikada33/istockphoto.com; p. 32: Brown Reference Group; p. 33: ESA/NASA/K. Sharon
& E. Ofek; p. 34: Brown Reference Group; p. 37: Stijn Peeters/istockphoto.com; p. 38:
Omrikon/Science Photo Library; p. 39: Kevin Drinkall/istockphoto.com; p. 40: Photographer's
Mate 3rd Class Andrew S. Garadi/U.S. Navy; p. 44: NASA; p. 45: NRAO/AUI/J. M. Uson

Library of Congress Cataloging-in-Publication Data

Salway, Andrew.
   Sound, Light, and Radiation / Andrew Solway.
      p. cm. -- (Exploring Physical Science)
   Includes index.
   ISBN-13: 978-1-4042-3746-9 (library binding)
   ISBN-10: 1-4042-3746-1 (library binding)
   1. Waves--Juvenile literature. 2. Vibration--Juvenile literature. 3. Radiation--Juvenile
literature. I. Title.
   QC157.S34 2007
   531'.1133--dc22

                                        2006036686

Manufactured in China

Contents

CHAPTER I

Traveling in waves

Sound, light, and radiation all travel in waves. First, though, we need to understand what a wave is. Have you ever seen an audience wave? It can be done in a line or in a large crowd in a sports stadium. If there is a group of people in a line, the person at one end of the line stands up and lifts their arms, then sits down. Just after that person stands up, the person next to him or her begins to stand up, too. Then the third person in the line stands, then the fourth, and so on. As each person in the line stands up then sits, it looks as if a ripple or wave flows from one end of the line to the other. But in fact, no one in the group has moved from his or her original position—each person stays in his or her place.

Researchers in Hungary have found that it takes about 30 people to start a wave in a sports stadium. The wave usually travels clockwise around the stadium, at a rate of about 20 seats per second.

What is a wave?

An audience wave is a good model for all kinds of waves, from ocean rollers to sound waves, and light waves. Any kind of wave carries energy from one place to another. A whisper may carry sound energy just a few inches through the air, while a giant star can send light energy across billions of miles of space.

In an audience wave, the movement travels along the line, but the people stay in one place—they just move up and down on the spot. In other kinds of wave, the energy moves, but it does not carry any **matter** along with it.

Spreading from the source

Any kind of wave has to come from a source of energy. The waves spread out from this source. You can see this happen if you drop a pebble into a still pool of water. The energy of the pebble sends out waves across the surface of the pool, in ever-widening circles.

Many kinds of wave

Waves occur naturally, but humans have put them to many uses. When we play music, we are creating sound waves. Flashlights, lamps, and laser beams are all sources of light waves. We also use many other kinds of wave energy, ranging from radio waves to gamma rays. You can find out about all these kinds of wave in this book.

 AMAZING FACTS

Waves from deep space

In 1977, two space probes, *Voyager I* and *Voyager II*, were launched into space by NASA, the U.S. space agency. The two probes flew by most of the planets in the solar system, and now are traveling into **interstellar** space. They still send information back to Earth daily, via radio waves. The radio signals travel at the speed of light 186,000 miles per second (300,000 kilometers per second). Even so, the signals from *Voyager I* take over 13$\frac{1}{2}$ hours to reach Earth.

CHAPTER 2

Anatomy of a wave

Any kind of wave is a vibration of some kind. This vibration can be up and down, or back and forth. It can be a vibration in the air, in water, in a solid—or in nothing at all. Some waves, such as light waves and radio waves, can travel through a **vacuum**. A very simple wave, such as the vibrations of a single, pure note, can be drawn as a diagram showing the changing movement of the wave. A simple wave of this kind is known as a **sine wave**. Sound, light, and other kinds of wave energy are sine waves.

 ## OSCILLOSCOPES

An **oscilloscope** is an instrument that can show changes in an electric current as a line on a screen. If a microphone is used to record a sound, the microphone will change the vibrations of the sound into "vibrations" in an electric current. If the sound is a single, pure note, it will show as a simple sine wave on an oscilloscope.

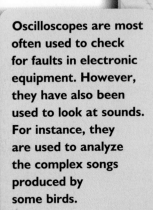

Oscilloscopes are most often used to check for faults in electronic equipment. However, they have also been used to look at sounds. For instance, they are used to analyze the complex songs produced by some birds.

Wavelength and amplitude

In a simple wave diagram, the same up and down motion repeats itself again and again. The size of one "repeat" is the distance between the **crests** (tops) of two successive waves. This is known as the **wavelength** of a wave.

The line along the center of the wave diagram marks the midpoint of the wave's vibration. The height that a wave vibrates above (or below) this midpoint line is known as the **amplitude** of the wave.

Wavelength and frequency

Another property of a wave is its **frequency**. The frequency of a wave is the speed at which it vibrates. Say, for instance, that you produce waves in a rope by waggling the end up and down. The frequency of the waves is the number of wave crests or **troughs** (low points) that pass a particular point on the rope every second. If you waggle the rope slowly, you will send only one or two waves each second, which is a low frequency. However, if you move the end of the rope up and down very fast, more waves pass along the rope each second (a higher frequency).

The frequency of a wave is related to its wavelength. If a wave has a long wavelength, then it has a low frequency—only a few waves pass by each second. However, a wave with a short wavelength has a higher frequency—many waves pass by in a second.

The large wave diagram shows the wavelength and the amplitude of a simple sine wave. The smaller diagram shows waves at two frequencies. The second wave is twice the frequency of the first.

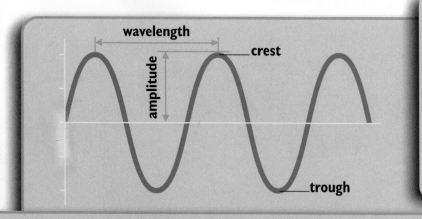

wavelength

crest

amplitude

trough

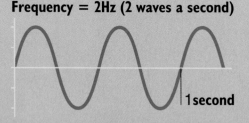

Frequency = 2Hz (2 waves a second)

1 second

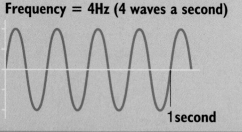

Frequency = 4Hz (4 waves a second)

1 second

Up and down, or back and forth?

Imagine a line of people, all standing close to each other, and the first person in the line pushes the next person. The second person falls against the third person in the line, but then manages to get his or her balance back. The third person, meanwhile, falls against the fourth person, and so on. A wave of movement passes down the line, but in a different way from the audience wave done at a sports event.

Audience waves and the "pushing" wave are illustrations of two basic types of wave. Light waves are up-and-down, or **transverse waves**, like the audience wave. Sound, on the other hand is a back-and-forth, or **longitudinal wave**.

Another way of showing transverse and longitudinal waves is to use a loose spring, the sort that is used to make "slinky" toys. If you fasten one end of the spring, sharply tap the side of the spring, you will produce transverse waves along it. If, instead, you quickly push the end of the slinky forward and then pull it back again, it will produce a longitudinal wave. In a longitudinal wave, the coils in one section of the spring are pushed close together, and the wave of compression travels down the spring.

transverse wave

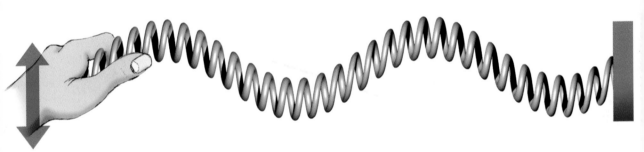

By moving the end of a loose spring up and down, you can produce transverse waves.

Combination waves

Some kinds of wave are a combination of both transverse and longitudinal waves. Waves and ripples in water are one example of this. The **atoms** (tiny particles) that make up the water move both forward and backward and up and down as a wave passes. The combination of both types of movement means that the atoms move in a circle.

Light waves have **wavelengths** and frequencies, just like sound waves.

longitudinal wave

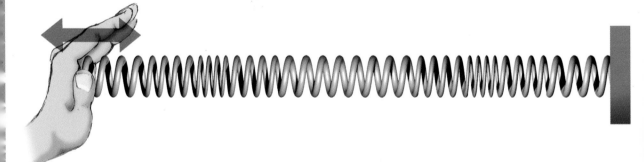

By moving the end of a loose spring in and out, you can produce longitudinal waves.

CHAPTER 3

Sound and hearing

If you put some grains of rice on a drum and then hit it, the rice bounces up and down. This happens because the drum skin vibrates when it is hit. As well as making the rice dance, the vibrations set off sound waves in the air. The sound waves are picked up by your ears, and you hear the sound of the drum.

 ## AMAZING FACTS

Silent vibrations

Not all vibrations produce sounds that we can hear. We cannot hear vibrations with a frequency less than about 20 **Hertz (Hz)** or more than about 20,000 Hz. Sound below the range of human hearing is called **infrasound**, and sound above our hearing range is known as **ultrasound**. Earthquakes, ocean waves, wind, and waterfalls all produce infrasound, as do some kinds of machinery. Elephants, cattle, and some birds can hear infrasound. Elephants use infrasound to communicate over long distances, while birds probably use it to help them navigate. Bats, whales, and dolphins can hear ultrasound far beyond our hearing range. We use ultrasound in instruments that can detect tiny cracks in metals, and in medical scanners used to monitor babies still in the womb.

Sound vibrations

The twang of a guitar string, the squeak of a rusty hinge, the clang of a bell, and the buzzing of a bee's wings are all vibrations that produce sounds. Most of the sounds we hear travel through the air to reach our ears. Although humans do not hear well in water, sound can travel through liquids, too. Aquatic animals have ears adapted to hear sounds underwater. Sounds also travel through solids. When we speak, we hear the sound of our own voice partly through vibrations traveling through our skull.

Sounds are **longitudinal waves**. Sound waves affect the **atoms** that make up the material the sound is traveling through. As a sound wave passes, the atoms move forward and then back again.

Pitch and volume

Not all sounds are the same. The **frequency** and **wavelength** of a sound affect its **pitch** (how high or low it is). Sounds waves with a high frequency and short wavelength are high-pitched, while sounds with a low frequency and long wavelength are low-pitched.

The **amplitude** of a sound wave relates to its volume. Sound waves with a high amplitude are loud, and small-amplitude sounds are quiet.

The huge skin on this Japanese taiko drum vibrates slowly, producing a very deep sound. The drummer uses thick, heavy sticks, which give a lot of energy to the vibration. This makes the drum sound very loud.

 HUMAN AND ANIMAL HEARING RANGES

Animals have widely different hearing ranges. Many animals can hear much higher sounds than humans, but few can hear lower sounds.

Animal	Hearing range (hertz)	
	low	high
Humans	20	20,000
Cats	100	32,000
Dogs	40	46,000
Horses	31	40,000
Elephants	16	12,000
Cattle	16	40,000
Bats	1,000	150,000
Grasshoppers and locusts	100	50,000
Rodents	1,000	100,000
Whales and dolphins	70	150,000
Seals and sea lions	200	55,000

Deafening decibels

The loudness of a sound is a measure of the amount of energy in the sound wave. If you hit a drum softly, it produces a quiet tapping sound, but if you hit it with a lot of energy, it will make a loud bang.

If a loud sound has too much energy, it can cause damage to your hearing. It is therefore important to be able to measure loudness, so that we can either avoid sounds that are too loud, or protect our ears from them. Sound is measured in units called **decibels**.

Reflecting and absorbing

An echo is a sound wave that has been reflected from a surface back to your ears, in the same way that light is reflected in a mirror. High walls, steep-sided valleys, and cliffs are often good places for echoes, because sound can reflect off the steep surfaces. As we will see on page 16, sound moves pretty fast. This means that to get a good echo, you need to stand a good distance from the reflecting surface. For instance, if you stand about 560 feet (170 meters) away from a wall or cliff, you will hear the echo about a second after you shout.

The noise of the jets on this aircraft carrier could seriously damage the ears of anyone working nearby. Ear defenders are packed with sound-absorbing material to reduce the level of sound reaching the ears.

THE DECIBEL SCALE

The decibel scale is not like the scale on a ruler. A sound of 20 decibels (dB) is not twice as loud as one of 10 dB—it is ten times as loud. A sound of 30 dB is ten times as loud again, or 100 times louder than a 10 dB sound. Loudness is measured this way, because a loud sound can be millions of times louder than a quiet one. The quietest sounds we can hear are around 10 dB, while sounds become painfully loud at about 130 dB.

Sound level	Example
160 dB	ears permanently damaged
130 dB	sounds become painful
120 dB	jet airliner taking off
110 dB	road drill
100 dB	front rows of concert
85 dB	heavy traffic
80 dB	vacuum cleaner
70 dB	sound of small orchestra
60 dB	busy department store
50-60 dB	normal conversation
20-30 dB	rustling of leaves, quiet whispers
10 dB	lowest limit of human hearing

Hard surfaces reflect sounds much better than soft ones. You may notice this if you move to a new house. When the rooms of your old house have been emptied, or before you unpack in your new house, the rooms echo and the noise level seems higher than normal. This is because there are no curtains, carpets, or soft furnishings to absorb sound waves, which **reverberate** (bounce) around the space.

An important sense

Hearing is one of our most important senses. The ear can be divided into three parts—the outer ear, middle ear, and inner ear. The outer ears (the flaps either side of the head) act like satellite dishes, collecting sound waves and focusing them on the auditory canal (the small opening that leads to the rest of the ear).

At the end of the auditory canal, sound waves coming into the ear meet the eardrum. This is a thin membrane stretched across the end of the canal. As sound waves hit the eardrum, they cause it to vibrate.

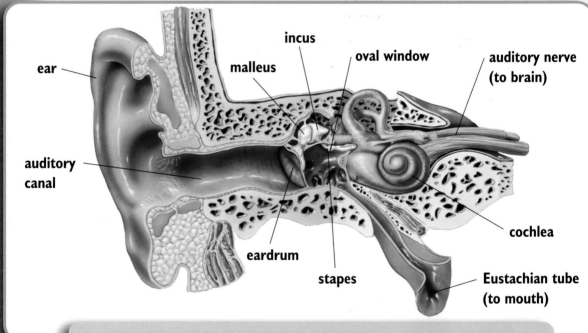

A sound enters the ear and travels down the auditory canal until it hits the eardrum. Small bones then amplify the vibrations. These vibrations cause tiny hairs in the cochlea to sway, which in turn sends nerve messages to the brain.

Amplifying the sound

The eardrum is the boundary between the outer and the middle ear. Spanning the middle ear are three tiny bones, called the malleus (hammer), the incus (the anvil), and the stapes (stirrup). The malleus connects with only a small area of the eardrum, so it concentrates and amplifies the movement of the eardrum. The incus and stapes bones act as levers, and amplify the sound vibrations even more.

The inner ear

The end of the stapes bone presses against another membrane, called the oval window. This is the boundary between the middle and the inner ear. The oval window connects with a long, coiled tube filled with fluid, called the cochlea. Down the center of the tube is a long membrane, the basilar membrane. The vibration of the oval window sends waves through the fluid of the cochlea, and these waves make the basilar membrane vibrate. The membrane is covered in tiny sensory hairs, which bend as the membrane vibrates. The bending of the hairs sends messages along nerves to the brain, which interprets the messages as sounds.

Many other mammals have large external ears that are better sound collectors than ours. They can also swivel their ears to pinpoint which direction a sound is coming from.

 AMAZING FACTS

Restoring hearing

Otosclerosis is a hearing disorder in which the stapes bone becomes fixed to the oval window. It can greatly reduce a person's hearing. However, surgeons can in some cases operate on the middle ear. They remove the stapes bone altogether, and replace it with an artificial stapes made from metal. This operation can restore hearing almost to normal levels.

The speed of sound

We learned on page 12 that if you stand about 560 feet (170 meters) from a cliff and shout, you should hear an echo about 1 second later. From this information, you can work out the speed of sound. In one second, the sound has traveled to the cliff and back again, 1,115 ft (340 m). So the sound travels at 1,115 ft (340 m) per second (or 760 mph). This is the approximate speed of sound in air at normal temperatures.

! AMAZING FACTS

Going supersonic

With the development of powerful jet engines after the World War II, it became possible for aircraft to travel faster than the speed of sound. When a plane travels faster than sound, it creates a shockwave in the air. This causes a loud sound like thunder, known as a **sonic boom**.

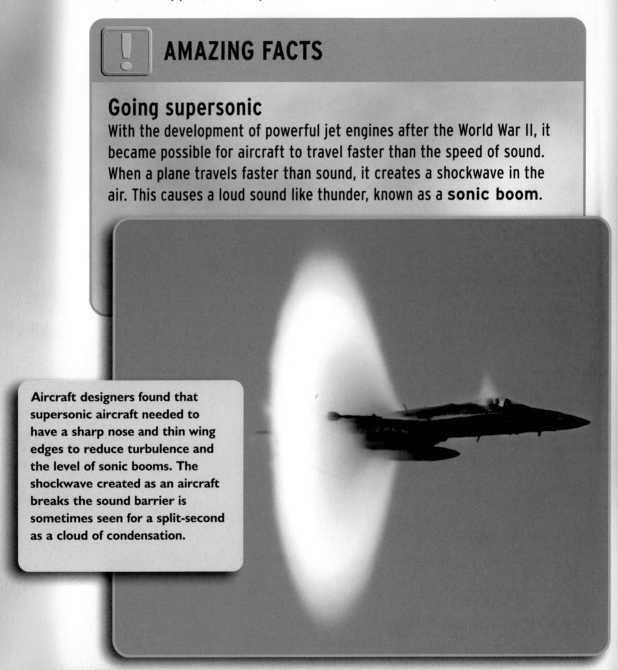

Aircraft designers found that supersonic aircraft needed to have a sharp nose and thin wing edges to reduce turbulence and the level of sonic booms. The shockwave created as an aircraft breaks the sound barrier is sometimes seen for a split-second as a cloud of condensation.

Sound travels at different speeds in other substances. For instance, it travels about three times as fast in water as it does in air, and about twelve times as fast in iron. However, sound waves must have something to travel through—they cannot travel in a **vacuum**.

Speed, wavelength, and frequency

If you know the speed that a wave travels at, it is possible to work out its **wavelength** from its **frequency**, or vice versa. For instance, the highest sounds humans can hear have a frequency of about 20,000 **Hz**. This means that 20,000 sound waves pass a particular point in one second. If we take the speed of sound as 1,115 feet (340 meters) per second, we know that the sound wave has moved 1,115 feet (340 meters) in that second. The 20,000 waves must be contained in a length of 1,115 feet (340 meters), so the wavelength works out as 2/3 inch (17 mm).

GREAT EXPERIMENTS

Boyle's jar

In 1668, the English scientist, Robert Boyle (1627-1691), with the help of his assistant Robert Hooke, conducted a series of experiments involving vacuums. In one experiment, Boyle and Hooke put a bell in a jar, with a mechanism to make the bell ring as the jar was turned around. They then pumped the air out of the jar. As the air was removed, the noise of the bell grew fainter, and then silent. The ringing could not be heard, because the sound waves could not travel through the vacuum inside the jar.

CHAPTER 4

The science of music

Music is different from other kinds of sound because it is organized. A musical tune, or melody, is usually made up of notes that are chosen to go well together, and they are sung and played in a particular rhythm.

Notes and scales

Most musical pieces use a special combination of notes. The **pitches** (notes) in a piece of music are organized into scales. A scale is a series of notes that span an octave, or eight ascending notes. If you listen to any kind of scale, you will hear that the first and last notes sound the same in some way, but one note is higher than the other. An **octave** is the gap between two notes that sound the same.

Measuring musical frequencies

The connection between the top and bottom notes of an octave is that the top note is twice the **frequency** of the bottom note. For instance, modern orchestras tune their instruments to a note (A) that has a frequency of 440 **Hz**. The A an octave below this will have a frequency of 220 Hz, while the one an octave above has a frequency of 880 Hz.

GREAT SCIENTISTS

Musical mathematics

The Greek philosopher and mathematician Pythagoras lived in the sixth century B.C. He and his followers studied how musical notes were related to each other, using vibrating strings. For instance, if a vibrating string is pressed in the center, to divide it in two, the two half-strings will produce a note an octave above the note of the full string.

The character of sounds

When a trumpet plays a tune, it sounds different from a violin, even when they play the same notes. If two notes have the same pitch, how can they sound different?

The answer is that most sounds are not a single frequency, but a mixture of several different frequencies. When a violin and a trumpet play the same note, the dominant frequency (the one that is loudest) is the same in both cases. But for each instrument there is a "supporting cast" of quieter frequencies, called **harmonics**, which give each instrument its character.

The sound waves produced by a viola (left) and a violin (right) will be slightly different, because they have different harmonics.

Plucking, hitting, and blowing

Different musical instruments produce sound in different ways. Instruments are broadly divided up into strings, percussion, and wind. Stringed instruments such as guitars and harps, produce sounds by making strings vibrate. In a harp, each string produces a particular note, which cannot be changed, but instruments like guitars have a fingerboard behind the string. By pressing the string against the fingerboard, the musician can make a shorter length of the string vibrate, producing a higher note.

 NATURAL SOUND PRODUCERS

Humans make sounds using the vocal cords. These are two flaps of tissue stretched across the airway near the top of your windpipe. In normal breathing, the vocal cords are relaxed and air can move easily past them. When you talk or make other noises, muscles stretch the vocal cords and the gap between them is reduced to a thin slit. As air passes through this slit, it makes the vocal cords vibrate. You can see how this works by pressing your lips together and then trying to blow though them. The air makes your lips vibrate and produce a sound.

As we push air through the vocal chords, we create sounds such as speech and song.

Percussion instruments vibrate when you hit them. Most drums and other kinds of percussion do not produce specific notes. However, instruments such as xylophones are known as **tuned percussion**, because they sound musical notes.

Trumpets, flutes, saxophones, and other instruments that you blow through are wind instruments. In a wind instrument, the player produces sounds by making the air inside the instrument vibrate. The player can change the note by opening or closing holes or valves in the instrument. The holes or valves shorten the amount of air that can vibrate, so opening them produces higher-**pitched** notes.

Natural amplifiers

Most instruments would produce quiet, flat sounds if they did not have "natural amplifiers" to amplify and enrich the sounds. The "amplifier" is called a **resonator**. The hollow body of a guitar or a violin is a resonator, as is the soundboard of a piano. If you compare the sound of an unplugged electric guitar, which has no resonator, with an acoustic guitar, which does, you will hear the difference a resonator makes.

A resonator relies on something called **resonance**. When, for instance, you play a note on a guitar, the air inside the resonator resonates, or vibrates in response to the vibration of the guitar string. This makes the note sound louder and richer.

A bird can sing two notes at once, because it has two sets of vocal cords. The vocal cords are further down the throat than in mammals, just below the place where the windpipe divides in two.

Recording sound

The very first sound recording was probably of "Mary Had a Little Lamb." It was made in 1877 by the U.S. inventor, Thomas Edison. To record the sound, he spoke into a large horn, which focused sound onto a thin sheet called a **diaphragm**. The diaphragm vibrated, causing a needle attached to it to vibrate, too. The needle pressed against a rotating cylinder covered with tinfoil, which recorded the sound vibrations as a "track" of indentations in the foil. This track could be played back using the same needle and horn as for recording.

Edison's tinfoil cylinders were soon replaced by wax cylinders, and then by plastic records. Then after World War II, a new kind of recording method was developed. Now tape recorders could record sounds onto plastic tape coated in microscopic magnetic particles. The recording head of the tape recorder magnetizes some of these particles but not others, producing a magnetic pattern on the tape that is a copy of the pattern of vibrations in the original sound.

Sound recording has come a long way since Thomas Edison and his tinfoil cylinder, pictured here in the late nineteenth century.

Getting the sound right

In a music hall or other large auditorium, sounds need to carry without losing their clearness. The best way to achieve this is to have a small amount of **reverberation**. In a recording studio, sound engineers try to cut out reverberation, and also any outside noises. To reduce reverberation, the walls of the studio are covered with sound-absorbent materials. Outside noises are cut out by double walls filled with sound-absorbent materials.

Digital recording

As computers became widespread in the 1970s and 1980s, **digital** sound recording was developed. In **analog** sound recordings (those described so far), the recording is a direct "copy" of the wave pattern of the sound. In a digital recording however, the sound wave is converted into a pattern of numbers. This is done by a process called **sampling**. The sound wave is "sampled" (measured) many times per second, and the measurements for each sample are stored in some way. On a CD, the measurements are stored as a pattern of "bumps" within the disk. In a computer memory, the numbers are stored either on a magnetic disk or within electronic circuits. The measurements are stored as **binary numbers**, so the storage method only needs two "numbers"—0 and 1.

Until digital recording became established, the best-quality recordings were made on large reels of magnetic tape. Studio tape recordings were as good quality as today's digital recordings, but digital has the great advantage that it is possible to copy recordings again and again without losing quality.

CHAPTER 5

Sight and light

It is easy to show that sound is produced by vibrations, and with an **oscilloscope**, you can actually see that sounds are waves. It is less obvious that light is a wave. Scientists first thought that light was a wave because it behaved like one. For example, light can be reflected and **refracted**, which are both properties of waves.

Light basics

Like sound, light waves can have a range of different **wavelengths** or **frequencies**. However, light waves are much smaller than sound waves. Between 400,000 and 700,000 light waves would fit in one-half inch, and light vibrates 400 to 750 trillion times per second.

Another difference between sound and light is that light does not need something to travel through. Light from the Sun travels almost 93 million miles (150 million kilometers) across the empty **vacuum** of space before it reaches Earth. However, we can never know what the Sun sounds like, because sound cannot travel through a vacuum.

Light sources

The Sun is the main source of light on Earth. Most other light sources are manmade. In the past, people used flaming flashlights, oil lamps, gas lamps, and other lights that worked by burning fuels. However, since the early twentieth century, electric lights have been the main light source in most countries. In the incandescent light bulb (the most common type), electricity flows through a thin, coiled wire called a **filament**. The electricity makes the filament so hot that it produces a bright, white light.

The filament of a light bulb reaches a temperature of almost 5,000 °F (3,000 °C). At this temperature, the filament would burn up in air. To avoid this, a light bulb has no air in it. However, it does contain a small amount of an inert (nonreactive) gas.

Laser light

If you look at a flashlight beam or a searchlight, you will see that the beam spreads as it gets farther from the source, producing a cone of light. As it spreads, the light beam also gets fainter. The beam from a laser is different. It stays pencil-thin, and it hardly fades at all. The reason for this is that lasers produce a very concentrated, pure kind of light called **coherent light**. A normal source of light produces light of many different wavelengths, and the light waves spread out in all directions. However, laser light produces light of just one wavelength, and the waves all travel in the same direction. What is more, the light waves all travel in step. The **crests** of all the light waves line up with each other, as do the **troughs**. It is this regular pattern that makes lasers so powerful.

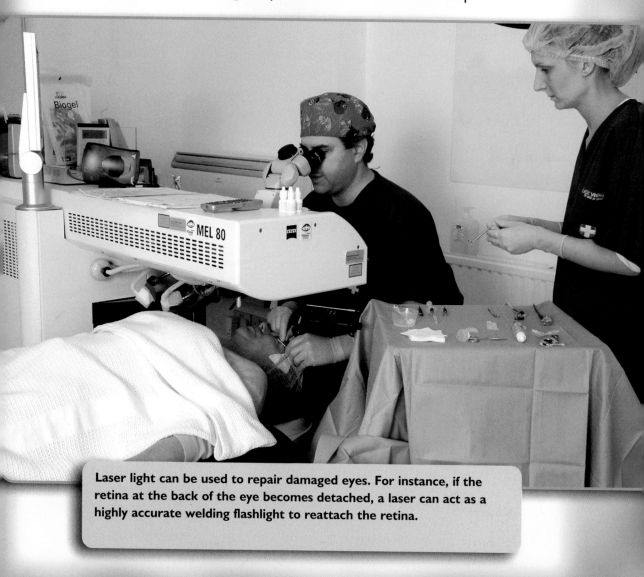

Laser light can be used to repair damaged eyes. For instance, if the retina at the back of the eye becomes detached, a laser can act as a highly accurate welding flashlight to reattach the retina.

Reflecting light

Without light from the Sun or other source, most objects would be invisible. This is because most objects around us do not produce light. When light hits an object, some of it is absorbed, and the rest bounces off the surface—it is reflected. **Transparent** materials, such as glass, transmit light (allow it to pass through).

Most objects reflect light in all directions—this is called **diffuse reflection**. This happens because even when an object is smooth to the touch, the surface contains many microscopic bumps and hollows. Light rays hitting the surface are deflected off in odd directions by these bumps.

A few very smooth surfaces, such as mirrors or highly polished metals, reflect light in a much more regular way, known as **specular reflection**. With specular reflection, the angle at which the ray of light hits the surface is the same angle that it will bounce off again in the other direction. It is because mirrors reflect light in such a regular way that we can see images in them.

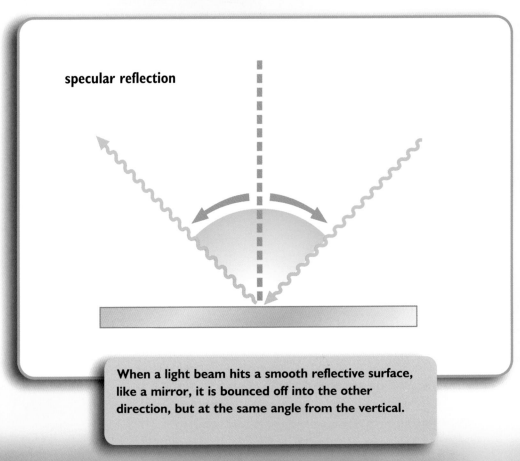

specular reflection

When a light beam hits a smooth reflective surface, like a mirror, it is bounced off into the other direction, but at the same angle from the vertical.

Reflections from the Moon

If you know the speed of light (see page 28), you can use a light to measure distances very accurately. One distance that has been measured this way is from Earth to the Moon. Space missions to the Moon in the 1960s and 1970s placed reflectors in several places on the Moon. It is possible to fire powerful pulses of laser light at one of these reflectors and detect the reflected light when it reaches Earth again. From measurements of the time the light takes for the round trip, it is possible to work out the Earth-Moon distance to within 1 inch (2.5 centimeters). The actual distance varies as the Moon orbits, but it averages around 217,000 miles (385,000 kilometers).

Refraction

Light travels in a straight line in empty space, or in air, or in still water. But as it moves from one transparent material to another, light can **refract**, or bend. The amount the light bends depends on what the two materials are. For instance, light moving from air into a diamond is bent more than light moving from air to water.

The amount that light refracts also depends on the angle at which the light beam meets the other material. A light beam meeting another material at a shallow angle bends more than if it meets the same material at a steep angle.

Lenses (see page 32) work by refracting light as it passes through them.

refraction

When a light beam hits a transparent surface, it is bent by that material as it passes through.

The speed of light

When you press the light switch on your bedroom wall, the whole room is lit immediately. When you turn on a powerful flashlight, the beam shoots out right away. Light does not seem to travel—it is just there in an instant. But this is just because light travels very, very fast, much too fast for our senses to notice it. The speed of light in a **vacuum** is approximately 186,000 miles per second (300,000 kilometers per second). At this speed, a trip to the Moon would take just over a second, and you could reach the Sun in about 8 minutes. In other materials, light does not move as fast as it does through a vacuum.

Sound and light

Compared to light, sound moves extremely slowly. Light travels almost 900,000 times faster than sound. The best-known example of this is when you see lightning flash during a thunderstorm. You may not hear the sound of thunder until several seconds after a lightning flash, because if the storm is some distance away, the thunder's sound will take several seconds to reach you. If the storm is half a mile or so away, for example, the light takes a fraction of a second (1/300,000th of a second) to reach you. However, the sound of the thunder takes about 3 seconds to travel the same distance (sound travels 3,350 ft. or 1,020 m in 3 seconds).

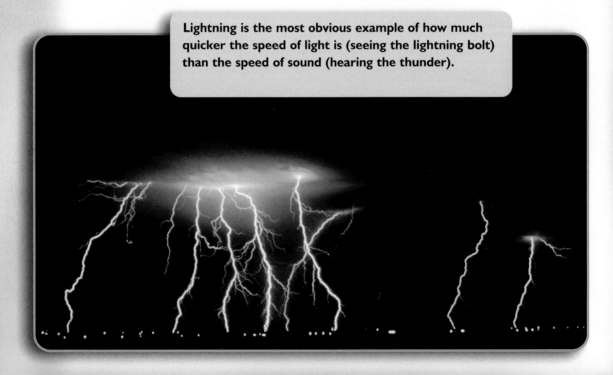

Lightning is the most obvious example of how much quicker the speed of light is (seeing the lightning bolt) than the speed of sound (hearing the thunder).

GREAT SCIENTISTS

Albert Einstein

The famous German scientist, Albert Einstein, showed that it is impossible to travel faster than the speed of light. In 1905, Einstein published one of his most important scientific papers, about the special theory of relativity. As part of this theory, he showed that as an object approaches the speed of light, the amount of energy needed to move it faster gets greater and greater. For an object actually to reach the speed of light, it needs an infinite amount of energy! Experiments with particle accelerators, which accelerate **subatomic particles** to very high speeds, have shown that this is true. It is possible to give tiny particles enough energy to approach the speed of light. However, no matter how much energy is put in, the particles never quite reach the speed of light.

A photograph of Albert Einstein, taken in 1931.

CHAPTER 6

Bouncing and bending

Reflection and **refraction** are two of the most useful properties of light. People have discovered ways to use reflection and refraction to put light to work in all kinds of **optical** devices.

Ways that mirrors reflect

A mirror is a piece of glass coated with a thin layer of silver on one side to make it a very good reflector. Flat mirrors reflect back light from objects in front of the mirror. The reflected rays of light seem to come from behind the mirror, so the image we see seems to be behind the mirror.

 AMAZING FACTS

Optical fibers

When light hits the surface of glass or some other **transparent** substance, it usually goes straight through. However, if it hits the glass at a shallow angle, the light reflects off the surface. Optical fibers take advantage of this property to send laser light signals along cables. An optical fiber contains two kinds of glass, one wrapped around the other. The light signal is sent along the inner glass core. When the light hits the outer glass wrapping, it is not absorbed, it just bounces off. The light reflects back and forth many times as it travels along the cable.

Optical fibers are at the heart of our communications networks. They can carry more information than electrical wires, and they carry it more quickly.

Mirrors can be curved instead of flat. A mirror that is curved inward like a bowl is concave; one that is curved outward like the surface of a ball is convex.

Concave mirrors

You can see how a concave mirror reflects light by looking at yourself in the bowl of a metal spoon. If you hold the spoon at arm's length, you will see yourself upside-down. As you move the spoon closer, at a certain point, your image turns right way up and becomes enlarged.

Shaving and makeup mirrors are concave, to give an enlarged image of your face. A more important use of concave mirrors is in telescopes. A large, curved mirror can collect light from a distant object and focus it to make an image of the object. Most large astronomical telescopes are made with concave mirrors.

Convex mirrors

To see how a convex mirror works—turn the spoon over! This time, the image in the mirror is always the right way up, and you appear smaller than you actually are.

Your image in a spoon looks distorted because of the way the spoon curves. But carefully designed curved mirrors have a range of uses. Convex mirrors give a wider than normal field of view, so they are used as security mirrors in stores. The wing mirrors on a car are also convex.

Lenses

Light is **refracted** when it moves from air to glass and back again. By making glass in particular shapes, it is possible to bend light in useful and predictable ways. This is what lenses do.

Two common kinds of lens are convex lenses and concave lenses. Both sides of a convex lens curve outward, while a concave lens curves inward on both sides.

Convex lenses

A convex lens concentrates and focuses light. If light from a distant object passes through a convex lens, the light converges (comes together) at a point, known as the **focal point**. The more a convex lens bulges, the more it bends the light, and the closer the focal point is to the lens.

If you hold a convex lens close to an object, it magnifies whatever you are looking at. A magnifying glass is a convex lens. If an object is farther away, the lens can produce an upside-down image of the object on a screen or a piece of paper. A camera uses convex lenses in this way to focus light on the film. Microscopes and binoculars also use convex lenses.

Convex lens

Focus (point at which rays meet)

Focal length

Convex, or converging lenses, bend light inward toward a focal point. Concave, or diverging lenses, bend light so that it spreads outward. The focal point of a concave lens is the point where these diverging rays would meet if they were straight.

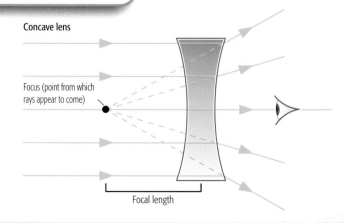

Concave lens

Focus (point from which rays appear to come)

Focal length

Concave lenses

Light passing through a concave lens spreads out, or diverges. If you look through a concave lens, things look smaller than normal. Concave lenses are used in spectacles (eyeglasses) for shortsighted people (see page 34).

Most cameras, telescopes, and other **optical** devices actually use groups of lenses rather than single ones. This helps to sharpen the image and to avoid producing colored fringes around the edges of images. Concave lenses are used in these combination lenses.

AMAZING FACTS

Bending light

On Earth, light does not seem to be affected by gravity. However, very **massive** objects should in theory bend light that passes near them. Astronomers have actually found examples of this happening. A very massive galaxy, or a cluster of galaxies, lying between Earth and a bright object, such as a quasar (a kind of galaxy with a very bright center), acts as a "gravitational lens," and bends the light from the quasar. The result is that we can see the quasar from Earth, even though it should be hidden by the galaxies that lie in between. Astronomers have been able to recognize this effect, because in some cases, the lens effect produces more than one image of the quasar.

The four bright "stars" near the center of the picture are all images of the same quasar. They are images produced by something called "gravitational lensing." Light from the quasar was bent by gravity as it passed close to a very massive group of galaxies between the quasar and Earth.

Seeing the light

We get 80 percent of our information about the world through our eyes. Light from the Sun or another light source falls on our surroundings, and is absorbed or reflected. Some of the reflected light enters our eyes and gives us our information about the world.

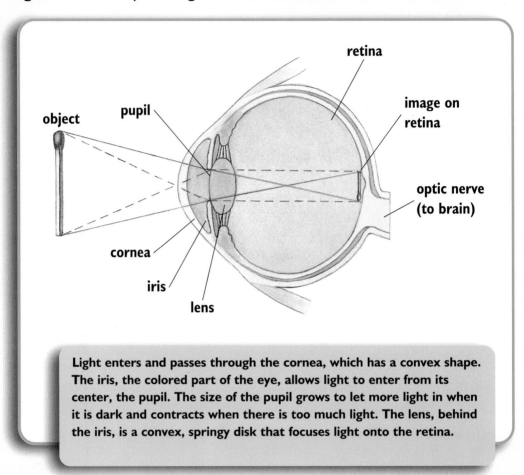

Light enters and passes through the cornea, which has a convex shape. The iris, the colored part of the eye, allows light to enter from its center, the pupil. The size of the pupil grows to let more light in when it is dark and contracts when there is too much light. The lens, behind the iris, is a convex, springy disk that focuses light onto the retina.

How eyes see

Our eyes are like a pair of digital movie cameras. In a digital camera, light is focused by a lens onto an array of millions of tiny sensors that are sensitive to light. Something similar happens in our eyes. Light coming into the eye is focused by the front part of the eye (the cornea) and the lens to produce an image of the outside world on the retina. The retina is a layer of cells on the inside of the eye that are sensitive to light. These light-sensitive cells send nerve messages to the brain when light falls on them. The brain uses this information to build up a picture of the outside world.

Autofocus and brightness control

The cornea does most of the **refraction** in the eye, but the lens is the eye's autofocus mechanism. The lens is elastic and can change its shape. Muscles attached to the lens can squash it to make it fatter, or stretch it to make it thinner. When the lens is fatter, it refracts light more strongly, which focuses images of close objects on the retina. When the lens is thinner, it refracts less strongly and focuses distant objects.

The eye can also work in a variety of light conditions. The pupil (the hole in the center of the eye) can expand or contract depending on light conditions. In bright light it contracts, to let in less light. In dim light, the pupil opens wide to let in more light.

 CORRECTING FOR ERRORS

Many people do not have perfect vision—some are shortsighted, while others are farsighted. Opticians can use spectacles or contact lenses to correct these eye defects.

In people with shortsightness, the eye focuses most objects short of the retina. This problem can be corrected with a concave lens, which spreads the light slightly before it enters the eye.

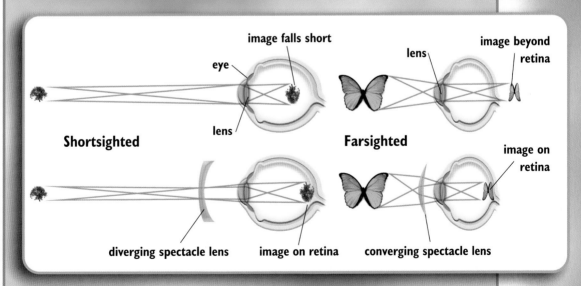

Shortsighted

image falls short
eye
lens

diverging spectacle lens
image on retina

Farsighted

lens
image beyond retina

image on retina

converging spectacle lens

In people who are farsighted, the eye focuses most objects beyond the retina. Farsightednesss can be corrected with a convex lens, which focuses the light slightly before it enters the eye.

35

CHAPTER 7

Adding color

Light, like sound, has a range of **wavelengths** and **frequencies**. For sound waves, the wavelength of a sound relates to its **pitch**. For light waves, wavelength, and frequency are related to color. The longest wavelengths of visible light are red, and the shortest wavelengths are violet. In between these, wavelengths are all the colors of the rainbow.

The range of wavelengths covered by visible light is quite small. Red light has a wavelength of about 700 nanometers, while the wavelength of violet light is about 400 nanometers. (A nanometer is a billionth of a meter.) Orange light has a shorter wavelength than red light, after which comes yellow, then green, then blue, then indigo, and finally violet. The wavelength or frequency of a light wave relates to its energy. Red light has the lowest energy, while violet light has the highest.

Two colors that are not part of a rainbow are black and white. Black is not a color—it is no light at all. White is not one color, but a mixture of all colors, or wavelengths, of light.

 GREAT EXPERIMENTS

Newton's prisms

The great English physicist, Sir Isaac Newton (1643–1727), lived for many years in Cambridge, England. In 1665, Newton bought a prism at the annual midsummer fair, and began experimenting with it. He used the prism to make a spectrum from white light, and this suggested to him that white light was in fact made up of many colors. However, he needed a second prism to prove this. Newton bought a second prism at the next midsummer fair, and placed it after the first one. The first prism split the white light into a spectrum, and the second one recombined it into white light again. This proved that Newton's idea was correct.

Splitting light

One way to demonstrate that white light is a mixture of all colors is to take a beam of white light and split it into its separate wavelengths. When the different wavelengths are spread out in this way, it is called a **spectrum**. This can be done with a prism. A prism is a piece of glass with a triangular cross-section. If you shine white light into one side of a prism, a spectrum or rainbow of colors comes out the other side.

A prism works because the glass in the prism **refracts** (bends) the different wavelengths of light in slightly different amounts. Red light is refracted least by the prism, and violet light is refracted the most.

Why do we see colors?

When light hits opaque objects (ones that are not **transparent**), some light is reflected and some is absorbed. How much light is reflected or absorbed depends on things such as the material the object is made of, and whether the surface is rough or smooth. However, what the object is made of can also affect the type of light that is absorbed. Most plants, for instance, contain a chemical called chlorophyll. Chlorophyll absorbs red, orange, yellow, blue, indigo, and violet light, but not green light. Because of the chlorophyll, most plants reflect only green light, and so they appear green.

Other objects appear colored for the same reason as plants—they absorb some **wavelengths** of light and reflect others. White objects absorb no wavelengths, so all colors are reflected. Black objects, on the other hand, absorb all wavelengths of light. Any number or combination of wavelengths can be reflected, which makes it possible for objects to have an almost infinite range of colors.

Seeing colors

Although there is a huge range of possible colors, our eyes detect these colors using just three different color sensors. Color vision relies on cells in the retina known as **cones**. There are three different kinds of cone cells, and each one is sensitive to a different range of wavelengths. One kind responds mainly to red light, one to green light, and one to blue light. The cones can detect many more colors than just red, green, and blue, because most colors stimulate more than one type of cone cell, so the colors "mix." For instance, if the green and red cones are stimulated by a particular kind of light, but the blue cones are not stimulated, the color is probably orange or yellow.

A special photograph shows the rods and cones of the eye. The rods (brown/yellow) are long nerve cells that respond to dim light. Cones (green) are shorter cells that detect color.

"SUPERCOLOR" VISION

Humans and other apes have the best color vision among mammals. Most mammals have only one type of cone cell and are blind to many colors. Birds, however, can see a range and complexity of colors much greater than our own. A bird's eyes have four different kinds of cone cell, rather than three. This allows them to separate colors more effectively than humans. Birds can also see a wider range of colors. Their eyes can see **ultraviolet** light, which has a shorter wavelength than violet light. Many reptiles and amphibians also have "supercolor" vision.

The bright-colored display plumage of birds like this male peacock probably look even more impressive to other birds, with their "supercolor" vision.

CHAPTER 8

Beyond light—radiation

The light that reaches us from the Sun is not limited to visible **wavelengths**. We saw on page 39 that birds can see **ultraviolet** light, which has a shorter wavelength than visible light. The heat we feel from the Sun is another kind of "light," known as **infrared**. In fact, there is a huge range of lightlike waves, which extends far beyond the infrared and ultraviolet. All these different kinds of waves are known as **electromagnetic radiation**.

Explaining electromagnetism

Electromagnetic radiation was discovered by the Scottish scientist, James Clerk Maxwell. His work built on the experiments of Michael Faraday and others, who showed that when electricity flowed through a wire, it produced a magnetic field around the wire, and that a moving magnet can generate an electric current.

Radio, television, radar (shown here), satellite commmunications, and hundreds of other devices that are essential parts of modern life, all developed out of Maxwell's work on electromagnetic radiation.

These experiments showed there was a close connection between electricity and magnetism—but what exactly was it? Maxwell wanted to turn Faraday's observations into mathematical equations that could explain and predict the behavior of electricity and magnetism.

In 1864, Maxwell produced a set of 20 linked equations that together explained the behavior of electricity and magnetism. Furthermore, Maxwell's equations predicted the existence of waves of oscillating (vibrating) electric and magnetic fields. With the help of some simple electrical experiments, Maxwell worked out what speed these electromagnetic waves would travel at. He found that they traveled at the speed of light. From this discovery, Maxwell concluded that light itself must be an electromagnetic wave.

Maxwell also predicted that it should be possible to generate electromagnetic radiation in the laboratory. Several scientists soon began to investigate this idea. The first to succeed was Heinrich Hertz (see box).

 ## GREAT SCIENTISTS

Heinrich Hertz

In 1887, eight years after James Clerk Maxwell died, the German physicist, Heinrich Hertz, proved Maxwell's prediction that electromagnetic radiation could be produced in the laboratory. Hertz used an electric circuit containing a device called a **condenser**—a pair of metal rods placed end to end, with a small gap between them. When the rods were given opposite electric charges, a spark jumped between them, and the electric current in the circuit rapidly oscillated (changed direction) back and forth. Hertz's condenser sent out radio waves, which were detected using another condenser.

When Hertz was asked if his radio wave apparatus could be useful, he said, "It's no use whatsoever." He could not have been more wrong! Most kinds of communications, including radio, television, and the Internet, use radio waves to carry information from place to place. Radio waves are also used in radar and many other inventions.

The electromagnetic spectrum

The electromagnetic **spectrum** is an extension of the visible spectrum of colored light. **Electromagnetic radiation** has an immense range of **wavelengths** and **frequencies**. At one end of the spectrum are radio waves, which can have a wavelength of several thousand miles. At the opposite end of the scale are gamma rays (rays produced by some radioactive materials), which can have a wavelength of one thousand trillionth of a just over a yard or a meter (1/1000,000,000,000,000 m)!

Uses of electromagnetic waves

Scientists and inventors have found many uses for electromagnetic radiation. One of the main uses is for communication. Because all electromagnetic waves travel at the speed of light, they can be used to send messages all around Earth, and beyond it. Radio waves, for instance, are used to send radio and TV broadcasts all over the world. They are also used to communicate with satellites orbiting Earth, and with space probes and manned space missions. Microwaves have a shorter wavelength than radio waves. They are used to carry cell phone calls, and for computers communicating through wireless networks. (You can, of course, also use microwaves to cook your meals.)

This diagram shows the full range of the electromagnetic spectrum, from radio waves to gamma waves. Just to the right of the center of the spectrum is visible sunlight.

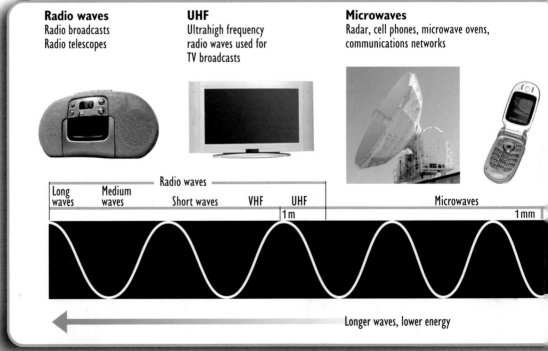

Radio waves
Radio broadcasts
Radio telescopes

UHF
Ultrahigh frequency radio waves used for TV broadcasts

Microwaves
Radar, cell phones, microwave ovens, communications networks

Radio waves

| Long waves | Medium waves | Short waves | VHF | UHF | | Microwaves |

1 m

1 mm

Longer waves, lower energy

GREAT EXPERIMENTS

Wilhelm Röntgen

X-rays were discovered by a German scientist, Wilhelm Röntgen. In 1895, Röntgen was experimenting with a cathode ray tube. This was a device for investigating the flow of electricity in a **vacuum**. On one particular November evening, Röntgen's experiment involved working in the dark. He noticed that a fluorescent screen at the other end of the laboratory was shining brightly. Röntgen was astonished—what was causing the glow? After some investigation, he realized that the cathode ray tube was giving off unknown rays, which were traveling across the room, lighting up the screen. Because the rays were unknown, he called them "X-rays."

Another use for electromagnetic radiation is to "see" where visible light cannot. X-rays are a very energetic kind of radiation, so they can pass through many materials that block light. Most body tissues are **transparent** to X-rays, but bones and teeth are not, so they show up clearly on X-ray pictures. Radar, which works using microwaves, is used in aircraft to "see" when normal visibility is poor (for instance, in fog or at night). Radar is also used for many other purposes. Air-traffic controllers, for instance, use radar to track aircraft at a distance, and police patrols use radar to check the speed of passing motorists.

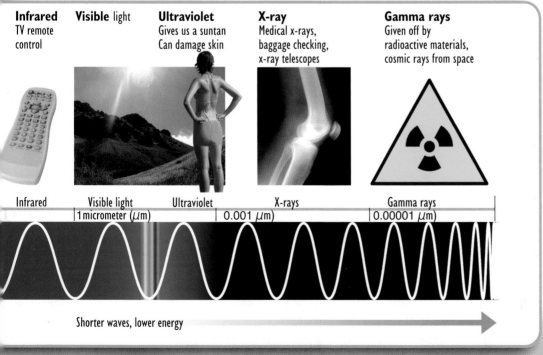

Infrared
TV remote control

Visible light

Ultraviolet
Gives us a suntan
Can damage skin

X-ray
Medical x-rays, baggage checking, x-ray telescopes

Gamma rays
Given off by radioactive materials, cosmic rays from space

| Infrared | Visible light | Ultraviolet | X-rays | Gamma rays |

1 micrometer (μm)   0.001 μm   0.00001 μm

Shorter waves, lower energy

Looking into space

People have studied the stars and planets for thousands of years. Since the invention of the telescope in the early 1600s, astronomers have been able to look farther and farther into space. Today, the Hubble telescope can see galaxies that are so incredibly far away from us that their light has taken billions of years to reach us.

Since the mid-twentieth century, astronomers have also been able to detect other kinds of **electromagnetic radiation** from space. Special telescopes that pick up different types of electromagnetic waves have made many new discoveries.

Radio telescopes

Telescopes to detect radio waves were the first specialist telescopes to be built. In the early 1960s, radio astronomers discovered some strange objects that looked like stars in visible light, but were giving off large amounts of radio energy. They became known as quasi-stellar objects or "quasars." Quasars are now known to be the centers of very distant galaxies that produce enormous amounts of energy.

Microwave telescopes

A small amount of microwave radiation comes from every part of space. It is known as **background radiation**. Telescopes to measure the background radiation have to orbit Earth, because Earth's atmosphere absorbs some microwaves. Careful measurements have shown that the background radiation is a remnant of a time just after the Big Bang (the beginning of the universe), when the whole of space glowed white hot.

The Hubble telescope orbits Earth as it takes photographs of deep space.

An image from the Very Large Array, a collection of 27 radio antennae based in New Mexico. This picture shows distant galaxy NGC1316 (center) devouring its small northern neighbor. The radio emissions caused by their encounter (the orange clouds) are 600,000 light years across each.

Infrared telescopes

Infrared telescopes pick up "heat rays" from the stars. To do this, they need to be in space, and shielded from the heat of the Sun. Infrared telescopes can "see" through thick clouds of gas and dust that block visible light. Most stars begin their lives in gas and dust clouds, so infrared telescopes have given us useful new information about the birth of stars.

X-ray telescopes

X-rays are high-energy radiation. They are produced when something is giving off a lot of energy. X-ray telescopes show up violent events in space, such as star explosions, and the huge amounts of energy produced as material falls into a black hole.

Messages from the stars

We have seen in this book that waves carry energy from place to place. Other types of wave can carry energy through solids, liquids, and gases, but only electromagnetic waves can travel through space. With modern instruments, we can pick up the faintest of electromagnetic signals from beyond Earth. Almost all the information we have about the universe comes from these messengers from distant stars and galaxies.

Glossary

amplitude the height of a wave. Amplitude affects the loudness of sound or the brightness of light.

analog using ever-changing electric currents or radio waves to carry information. In recording, an electric "copy" of a sound wave.

atoms the extremely tiny particles that make up all substances.

binary numbers numbers that use only the digits 1 and 0. In binary numbers, 2 is 10, 3 is 11, 4 is 100, and so on. Computers use binary numbers.

crest the top of a wave.

digital using digits (numbers) to carry information.

electromagnetic radiation light, radio waves, microwaves, infrared, ultraviolet, X-rays, and gamma rays are all types of electromagnetic radiation.

frequency the number of waves that pass a particular point every second. A wave with a short wavelength has a high frequency, and vice versa.

harmonics other notes, or overtones, that sound when a note is played on an instrument.

hertz (Hz) the unit for measuring frequency. One Hz = 1 wave per second.

infrared radiation that is just below the red end of the visible spectrum.

interstellar literally, "between stars," meaning deep into space.

longitudinal wave a wave made up of areas of compression and expansion, rather than highs and lows.

massive having a high mass. The mass of something is a measure of how much matter ("stuff") it contains.

matter any physical substance, whether solid, liquid, or gas.

optical relating to sight or vision.

oscilloscope an electronic device that can be used to visualize sound waves on a screen.

pitch how high or low a sound is.

refraction the bending of light when it moves from one transparent material into another.

resonance when a sound or other vibration sets off a sympathetic vibration in another object or material.

reverberation all the small echoes produced when sound bounces off the walls of an enclosed space.

sine wave a simple up-and-down wave shape.

spectrum a range. The visible spectrum is the range of colors that make up white light—red, orange, yellow, green, blue, indigo, and violet.

subatomic particles the tiny particles that make up an atom.

supersonic over the speed of sound.

transparent allowing light to pass through.

trough the bottom of a wave.

ultraviolet radiation that is just beyond the violet end of the visible spectrum.

vacuum nothingness. On Earth, we are surrounded by air, but a vacuum contains no air, gas, or any other material.

wavelength the length of a single wave. The wavelength of a sound affects its pitch, while the wavelength of light determines its color.

Further information

Books

Amazing Optical Illusions, Al Seckel. Firefly Books, 2004.

Encyclopedia of Space, Heather Couper. Dorling Kindersley, 2003.

Horrible Science: Sounds Dreadful and Frightening Light, Nick Arnold. Scholasitc Hippo, 1998, 1999.

Light and Sound (Young Oxford Library of Science), Johnathan Allday. Oxford University Press, 2002.

Science Files: Light and Sound, Chris Oxlade. Wayland, 2004.

Science Investigations: Light, John Gorman. Wayland, 2006.

Science Investigations: Sound, Jack Challoner. Wayland, 2006.

Web sites

Due to the changing nature of Internet links, The Rosen Publishing Group, Inc., has developed an online list of Web sites related to the subject of this book. This site is updated regularly. Please use this link to access the list: www.rosenlinks.com/ps/waves/

Index